GO BOLD!

~The Nail Polish Challenge~

Blasting Through Your Comfort Zone

Amy Head, LCSW

Chervoti,
Keep rocking!
Keep BELIEVing,
and always
GO BOLD! :)
Amy

Acknowledgements

Until near the end of 2015, the only person who knew that I was writing this book was me! It was a surreal experience to be living something and breathing life into something each and every day, knowing that not another human soul had a single clue. One might think that, because of this, there would be few people to acknowledge in this journey, but, that is far from the truth! There are so many thanks to be shared! My gratitude is overflowing! I must specifically mention the following:

My Facebook community: This book cover design is because of all of YOU who helped me design and decide which cover was best suited for this book! You were so invested in this process, offered so many great insights and ideas, and were so excited for me and this project! Your help and support meant so much to me! Thank you to each and every one of you.

The staff at Panera Bread in the Avenues of East Cobb in Marietta, GA: Panera was my writing laboratory. I would camp out in "my" booth, put my ear buds in, and get to work. The staff members were always supportive and encouraging as I worked on my "project." Panera became my personal "Cheers," where everybody knew my name, and I knew theirs.

Thanks, Panera, for being an awesome "satellite office" for my work.

My clients: I work with people who are in the midst of difficult times. They want things in their lives to be better, but they question if that can ever happen or if they even deserve it. To me, these folks are pictures of strength and resilience. They have gone through so much and continue to persevere. My clients are an unending source of inspiration. Thank you to all of you!

Jessica Asbell: Jessica is our awesome children's minster at our church and is one of the most detailed-oriented people I know! When she agreed to be an outside reader for me, I knew I would be in great hands! Jessica, thanks so much for all of the help, ideas, and detailed edits! You rock!

Noelle Abent: Noelle is a Reiki Master, a friend and colleague of mine. She spent many hours as one of the editors for this book. Her eye for detail caught things that I know I wouldn't have seen. Noelle, thank you so much for your help and awesome energy!

Michelle Pace: Michelle is an amazing friend and photographer who came to the rescue for me in a big way. After my completely amateur attempt at taking pictures of the nail polish bottles on the bathroom counter in my house, I asked Michelle if she would photograph these bottles for me. Wow! She made them look like something right out of a professional magazine. Michelle, thank you so much for your mad skills!

My Mastermind Group: More will be said about the people in this group later, but, I have to take a moment to thank them now. I put this group of five people together a couple years ago to serve as motivation, accountability, and guidance for each other as we work to grow our businesses! It is my sounding board for my greatest desires, fears, and challenges related to professional life. When I revealed late in the fall of 2015 that I had been working on this book, their responses were more enthusiastic and supportive than I could have imagined. Since then, they have helped me so much. They have been outside readers and editors, generated title ideas, provided feedback on content and design, and kept me accountable so that I would not run out of steam. Words cannot express my gratitude to Lynn Abent, Jan Cutini, Mike Dunham and Susan Palace! Thank you for your friendship, mentorship, inspiration, and so much more!

Mike Dunham: As a part of my Mastermind group, I have to take another moment to thank Mike. Mike and I met about 6 years ago through a weekly networking group. We have both served as leaders and referral partners within the group and are still doing so as of this writing. Mike is an attorney and has also authored two books. I had the privilege of being an outside reader for Mike's second book and had the amazing experience of seeing that project come to life. Little did I know then that he would end up becoming an outside reader, and editor, for me, as well as an integral part of putting together the layout and design of this book. Thank you, Mike, for being there for me every step of the way!

My Mom and Sister and My Dad: My Dad, Stuart, passed away in October of 2002. That was a tough time for the three of us girls. We watched him go through, and lose, his battle with cancer in his early 60s. He had so much more he wanted to do, and so much more he wanted to give, but, he was not given the chance. So, my mom, Loretta Weisberg, and my sister, Julie Weisberg, and I picked up the torch and kept running the race in his memory and honor. Over the years, the three of us have kept my dad's entrepreneurial spirit alive in so many ways, from starting our own businesses, to writing books, to creating unique opportunities for success. Through it all, we have supported and encouraged each other in all of these efforts. My mom and sister are my biggest cheerleaders, always sharing what I am doing with those they know! Thank you so much, Mom and Julie, for providing a safe, fun and inspirational place to land!

My Daughter and Son: When I told our kids, Jenna and Joshua, about this nail polish journey, they were both surprised – very surprised! They couldn't believe that I had been working on this all year long without telling anybody! They couldn't believe that I hadn't leaked it to a family member, a friend, or even more unbelievably, Facebook! My kids know me well, and they know that I love to communicate and keep people connected and informed. I think it shocked them that I kept such good wraps on something that I was so invested in for a whole year. Upon learning of all of this, they couldn't have been more supportive or encouraging. They even began brainstorming ways for me to market the book. I am so proud of these two and the young adults they are becoming. There are not enough words to convey my deep love and pride for them. Thank you, Jenna and Joshua, for loving me and for being the best kids a mom could hope for!

My Husband: Kevin and I have been married close to three decades. In all that time, I can't think of anything that was harder for me to do than to keep this nail polish journey from him. It was awkward to invest myself in something without him knowing about it. I explain more about this later. For now, let's just say that once I revealed what I had been up to all year, Kevin was shocked. He wasn't shocked that I had done something like this. He knows I always have a bunch of crazy ideas going at one time. I think, like the kids, he couldn't believe I didn't reveal any of this earlier. Once I told him about this project, his support, encouragement, and belief in me were immediate. Kevin has always believed in me, especially at times when I barely believed in myself. His smile and gentle nature give me the faith to believe that I can do or be anything I set my mind to. While he didn't know that this project was happening, it would not have happened at all if I didn't know, in the back of my mind, that he would be my greatest fan! Thank you, Kevin, for loving me as I am, for inspiring me and encouraging me to be who I hope to be!

There is no way to limit gratitude. I am so thankful to everyone who has been a part of my life through my work, my professional network, my church, my family, and my social media network connections. You were inspiring me, challenging me, motivating me, encouraging me, and supporting me all the way!

Meaning in life, for me, comes when you invest in others. It comes from when you are lucky enough to have the privilege, honor and opportunity to share who you are and what you do with those whom you love and who love you back. Much love and thanks to everyone mentioned above! This book would not have happened without you!

Introduction

How it all began

As 2014 was drawing to a close, I was thinking about what I might do differently in 2015. I have never been much for making New Year's resolutions, but I was feeling like I really wanted to be more intentional about something that year.

It was a year of anticipating change for our daughter, who would graduate from high school in May of 2015 and would head off to college a couple months later. She was still deciding which school she wanted to attend, but she would definitely be going somewhere.

It was a year of anticipating change for our son, who would get his driver's license at the end of January 2015. He would soon be able to drive himself everywhere that we used to drive him. He wasn't leaving home for college like our daughter, but, he was going to have the ability to leave home more often for school, sports practices and games, or just to hang out with friends.

It was a year of anticipating change for my husband, who would be considering a job change. He was in a great full-time job and was also serving on our church staff part-time. He was also working with me in our counseling practice.

However, he would soon have the opportunity to make a switch from his current full time job to serving our church full time. We didn't know what he would decide. What we did know was that one way or another, professional, personal and financial changes were on the horizon.

It was a year of anticipating change for me, too. I was helping my family manage all of these upcoming changes in their lives as well as continuing to manage the growth and development of my two businesses. I also created, organized and facilitated an entrepreneurial Mastermind Group. This group was made up of like-minded business professionals, hand-picked by me, whose purpose was to meet together on a regular basis to challenge, support, encourage, and ultimately help each other to have the confidence and strategies to grow our businesses beyond our wildest dreams.

All of this change was coming. All of this change was good. All of this change got me thinking: is there some sort of good change that I should do or that I need to initiate just for me, not for my family or for my businesses, but, just for me? Is there some sort of goal, vision, and/or outcome that I would want to strive toward in order to make 2015 a meaningful and banner year?

And, then, it hit me.....Nail Polish!

I was sitting down to polish my nails the Christmas week of 2014. This was not unusual for me as I always love to get in the spirit of the holidays with my jingle jewelry, my "pretty" (ugly) Christmas sweaters, my socks adorned in winter and holiday scenes and, of course, my festive nail polish. I had pulled out some red nail polish and some green and red glitter nail polish to go on top of the red to make my nails even more sparkly! I only wore this glittery nail polish during the holidays. I remember thinking to myself how I probably would never wear this type of glitter nail polish unless it was a special occasion where it "made sense," like on Christmas or New Year's Eve. This type of glitter nail polish seemed kind of obnoxious or bold for someone like me because of my personal style. I would consider my personal style to be more on the "classic-basic" side. I tend to gravitate toward more of the natural, neutral, earthy colors or classic black, navy, cream and white for my clothes. My jewelry box consists of a variety of silver and gold with some color accents. I wear more solids than prints. I would say that my classic-basic style also trends toward clothes that are more tailored in their fitting, especially for work/professional purposes.

While I was polishing my nails that day of Christmas week, putting the glitter coat on top of the red coat of polish, I started wondering what it would be like if I wore different colors of nail polish on a regular basis. Not just different colors that I would feel "comfortable" wearing, but different colors that I wish I would wear but probably wouldn't because they weren't "me!"

I started going through my collection of nail polish bottles. Here's a snapshot of what I had:

As you can see, I had lots of red, red-orange, light rose, light mauve, light beige, and a few glitter polishes for those special, festive occasions. This was as "bold" as it got! These were all pretty colors but, they were limited within a certain area of the color wheel. They were safe colors. They were familiar colors. They didn't draw attention. They were colors that said, "I am professional," or "I am together with a splash of fun." They were predictable, acceptable and expected, at least from me and my personal style.

As I thought about the colors that I owned, I realized how different they were from some of the colors that I might like to wear but probably wouldn't wear because they seemed too bold, youthful, or unprofessional. The colors I was thinking about were colors like chocolate brown, black, white, blue, green, purple, pink, orange and ALL of the different shades of these colors.

What would it be like to be bolder in my color selection? What would it be like to have other people seeing my hands with these bolder colors gracing my fingernails? Would I feel weird? Would I feel uncomfortable? Would I feel judged? Would I feel odd?

What would it be like to be BOLD or to GO BOLD in 2015?

It was at this moment that I knew exactly what would become my intentional commitment for 2015! Out with the OLD and in with the BOLD! I would change my nail polish every week to a color that would be different, new, unusual, and even uncomfortable for me to wear! I would take time each week to survey the various nail polishes at the store and pick out next week's color. I thought about the financial cost of this type of

New Year commitment, and realized that I could buy one new nail polish per week for less than the cost of a weekly meal at my favorite office away from the office, Panera Bread. So, the week after Christmas, I made my first investment in a new nail polish purchase. The commitment to GO BOLD in 2015 was on!

I recorded the nail polish color of the week in my calendar planner. At the end of each month, I lined up all of the nail polishes for that month on the bathroom counter and reflected on how the weeks and month, overall, had gone wearing these colors. I was filled with many thoughts, feelings and insights. I thought about what might have been different for having worn them. I thought about what might have been different had I not intentionally been bolder than usual!

52 weeks have come and gone, and I now have 52 weeks of going BOLD! What did that mean? What did I experience? What did I learn in these 52 bold weeks? Let's find out!

January

Week 1:   OPI (*red*)
Week 2:   WET AND WILD - ICED SUGAR COOKIE (*light pink*)
Week 3:   REVLON – CHOCOLATE TRUFFLE (*brown*)
Week 4:   FASHIONISTA (*blue*)

January, Week 1
OPI (red)

This was not a stretch for me, as red is a color that I wear at the holidays. Being the first week of January, it still felt like the holidays. But, the polish was a more expensive brand than I would normally buy. On a sub-conscious level, I think I was trying to prove my commitment to this challenge by paying a little more for the first polish of the year even though I stuck with a familiar color! There is not really too much else to say at this point, except that I am taking in and embracing this idea of change, of going bold, and I am proceeding with deliberate and gradual steps forward.

I am...embracing this idea of change, of going bold...

January, Week 2
WET AND WILD - ICED SUGAR COOKIE
(light pink)

This color was not as big of a stretch for me either as it was a color that fell into my color wheel, but, it was a change from the bold red of the previous week. I think it was still warming up to the challenge in a sense. I knew I was committed, but, I was finding that going too bold at first was a bit too much for me. That is pretty typical to my personality. I tend to test the pool water quite a bit before jumping in. I tend to taste a small bite of food that is not familiar to me instead of just taking a big bite. I was warming up! I wasn't having second thoughts, but I was just a little slow to go bold! I wasn't reneging on my commitment which, again, is also pretty typical to my personality. If I make an intentional commitment to something, I will follow through. I will keep my word.

I will follow through.
I will keep my word.

January, Week 3
REVLON – CHOCOLATE TRUFFLE (*brown*)

This was the first color outside of the spectrum for me, and I loved it! Not only was it chocolate brown, which I thought looked very cool, but it was also scented and smelled just like chocolate! Who knew that there was a nail polish out there that smelled like its color name? I love chocolate! So, this was the first perfect bold choice for me – it looked good, it smelled great, and it made me feel bold! I noticed myself looking down at my polished nails many times a day and feeling awesome. I felt different, more confident, and more fashionable. Ahhh – it's amazing what a little chocolate can do!

I noticed myself...
feeling awesome.

January, Week 4
FASHIONISTA (*blue*)

This color brought about a similar reaction within me as the chocolate truffle from the week before. I was a little more self-conscious because I had never worn any shade of blue on my nails. But, again, I was very aware of my polished nails and found myself gaining a sense of empowerment whenever I observed them. As was the case last week, I found myself glancing at my fingernails many times a day, almost as if I was taking in a little extra personal power with each look. It's funny how a simple color can have such a poignant impact. The blue was calming and bold at the same time.

It's funny how a simple color can have such a poignant impact.

Parting Thoughts

January was the beginning of something new and different for me. It was the start of a personal challenge, one that was only known to me. That, in and of itself, was strange, just knowing that if I continue with this the way I have in my mind, there will be potentially 52 weeks where I will be intentional in a specific area in my life yet nobody but me will have any idea. This is going to be interesting!

This month, I began the process of moving from traditional and comfortable, to new and exciting. The start to going bold was slow and incremental, maybe even slower than I had hoped or anticipated, but it happened! I felt self-conscious at first and, then self-assured by the end of the month. Going Bold had begun!

February

Week 1:   RIMMEL – MIND THE GAP (*light blue*)
Week 2:   WET AND WILD – GRASPING AT STRAWBERRIES (*red*)
Week 3:   WET AND WILD – BE MORE PACIFIC (*blue-green*)
Week 4:   BE MORE PACIFIC (*half the week*); NO POLISH (*half the
          week*)

February, Week 1
RIMMEL – MIND THE GAP (*light blue*)

This was the first "fun" color for me – maybe a little too fun! Until now, I felt bold and "professional." This time, though, I realized that I felt a potential need to hide my polished nails. It was weird. In some of my professional settings, I found myself second-guessing this color, even wishing that I had chosen something less bold. I was judging myself and worrying that colleagues might be judging me, too. Most people who know me know that I am a pretty nonjudgmental person. Because of that, I "felt" like if people thought my color choice was inappropriate or odd, they would probably be supportive of me anyway. Regardless of that, I was judging myself. I had to "tough out" some situations by talking to myself and reminding myself that the uncomfortable feeling was exactly why I was doing this challenge. It was time to be bolder and live each day to the fullest with no limits!

It was time to…
live each day to the fullest
with no limits!

February, Week 2
WET AND WILD - GRASPING AT STRAWBERRIES
(red)

Not only was this color a bolder and brighter shade of red for me, but it was also a brand that I had not purchased before. "Wet and Wild" was an interesting addition to this challenge because these color selections were getting more wild as the weeks progressed. Making it through the awkwardness of last week actually allowed me, I think, to feel less awkward about this bright red. I found myself more willing to allow this color to be seen in my professional circles. The color felt fun and vibrant. I have to confess, though, that this was the week of Valentine's Day. So, what seemed like a new level of confidence for me might not have been as much about confidence as it was about being "okay" with this brighter color because it was during Valentine's Day festivities. Either way, I wore it!

I found myself more willing to...be seen in my professional circles.

February, Week 3
WET AND WILD – BE MORE PACIFIC
(blue-green)

My boldest color to date! I was proud of myself! Not only was I going to wear this color in my professional settings, but I was also going to wear it to jury duty! Yes! My whole life, I had wanted to serve on a jury, and, now, I would be serving during the week of my most bold nail polish! I was doubly proud of myself for not being intimidated to serve while wearing my boldest polish! I couldn't have been more excited! And, then....it happened! It SNOWED here in Atlanta! Now, I LOVE snow but I did not want this snow to postpone jury duty. Luckily, it didn't. I reported to the courthouse on the first two days only to find out that I would not be selected to serve. I was disappointed – I wanted to serve and show off my nail polish! Snow or no snow, show or no show, one thing was for sure – I was definitely in the groove of this bold challenge!

I was definitely in the groove of this bold challenge!

February, Week 4
BE MORE PACIFIC (*half the week*)
NO POLISH (half the week)

Due to the inclement weather of the previous week, I decided to keep the same color of nail polish on for the first half of this week so that I could wear it to some of the activities that got cancelled. I felt good. I felt bold. By about mid-week, I was ready to take on another color. Instead of starting a new color then, I decided to go without polish for the remainder of the week. I figured this would be a good chance to go back to what I was used to, no polish, and see how it felt after a couple months of different colors. I have to say, I felt a little bare, a little boring, a little blah. I was surprised that what used to be the "usual" for me now seemed strange. I remember thinking that I could not wait until Sunday or Monday to take on the next color!

> *...what used to be the "usual" for me now seemed strange.*

Parting Thoughts

February was a month of settling into the bold. I had mixed emotions at times, and found myself on the verge of judging myself, or second-guessing what I was doing, or worrying about how I was being perceived. As I pushed through all of that, I began feeling more and more comfortable and more confident.

The temptation to throw in the new towel of going bold for the old towel of comfort and familiarity was real. It was a struggle. What I found, though, was that by standing tall, staying true, and talking myself through the situations, I began to conquer my fears or insecurities! Having the courage to take on those significant struggles, even when it seemed that the courage wasn't always there, allowed me to take big steps forward!

March

Week 1: REVLON – VIXEN (*maroon*)
Week 2: PURE ICE – SATIN RIBBON (*light pink*)
Week 3: SINFUL COLORS – SAVAGE (*aqua blue*)
Week 4: REVLON – BORDEAUX (*wine red*)
Week 5: SINFUL – BLAH BLAH (*dark tan*)

March, Week 1
REVLON – VIXEN (*maroon*)

This color was awesome! It felt bold and familiar while, at the same time, it was sort of in my wheel house of colors but with a little more power! I felt great wearing it! I felt professional, confident, and powerful! It was awesome to get color back on my nails. Several days of not wearing polish was tougher than I thought it would be. During those days, I felt unfinished and a bit less secure. It was weird because I had spent most days of the previous year with no polish and never really gave it a second thought. But, after wearing various colors for a number of weeks, I felt like something was missing. So, this color was a perfect way to get back on the color wheel! My husband, Kevin, and I went to see the musical, "Wicked" this week. I remember many times throughout that evening feeling pretty "wicked" myself as I was growing in my boldness!

I felt professional, confident, and powerful.

March, Week 2
PURE ICE – SATIN RIBBON (*light pink*)

While this was the lightest of all of the colors since starting this challenge in January, I liked it! One thing I did was put on three coats of polish, and that made it stronger to me. It was a color that actually made me feel chic and stylish. I wore jewelry that complimented the color, including pearls on some days and brown leather bracelets on other days. This was a color that could be dressed up or down easily, and I liked that. It was cool to wear and more subdued, yet still feel bold and strong. This color fit my classic style. Instead of thinking of my style as "classic-basic" like I usually do, I found myself thinking of it as "classic-bold." That was pretty awesome!

It was cool to wear and more subdued, yet still feel bold and strong.

March, Week 3
SINFUL COLORS – SAVAGE (*aqua blue*)

It was time for a blue color again and the name of this one made me feel like, "YES! Let's GO!" I had no apprehensions this time like I did the first time that I wore a shade of blue. I was looking forward to wearing a color called "savage" – I mean, how much bolder can you get? This was interesting because I remember feeling like the color didn't quite measure up to the name. I found myself wishing that the shade of blue was stronger and bolder than it actually was. Hmmm...this was definitely different for me! I started out this challenge feeling shy and second-guessing the colors that were a bit bolder than what I felt like was me. Now, here I was feeling somewhat disappointed in the color not being bold enough. I guess a shift was happening within me.

I guess a shift was happening within me.

March, Week 4
REVLON – BORDEAUX (*wine red*)

This was another one of those colors that was not only bold in color but was also bold in scent. It actually smelled like red wine! This was funny to me considering that I don't drink – at all! So, this time, what I found was that I was not self-conscious about the color one bit. Instead, I was wondering if others could "smell" the wine on me – LOL! It was a pretty strong scent. You could even say the scent was stronger than the color! But, I wore this color proudly, and nobody ever said a word about the smell! It was a fun color to wear. Like the chocolate truffle color from January Week 3, I liked that the color spoke to more than one of the five senses. It kept me engaged on several levels. It felt and looked great!

I liked having a color that spoke to more than one of the five senses.

March, Week 5

SINFUL – BLAH BLAH (*dark tan*)

I was looking forward to this color. It was more within my original wheelhouse. But, when I put it on, I felt exactly like the name of the color – "BLAH!" Wow! This was surprising to me! From the bottle it looked like a darker tan, but, on me it looked kind of like clay. It didn't really do anything for me. I felt blah! I had to push through this color the entire week. It was tough! I could have removed it and chosen another one, or I could have polished over it with something different. I considered both options. I decided to stick to and trust the process, to sit with it and experience this halt in the bold forward movement. It was interesting that, unlike February Week 1, where I had to push through to hang in there with a bolder color, this time I was pushing through to hang in there with a blander color. It was a great reminder of how far I had come. For the first time, I thought to myself, "I may never go back to 'blah'."

> *I decided to stick to and trust the process.*

Parting Thoughts

March was the first month for actually "feeling" bolder! Rather than simply settling in to the idea of going bold, I felt like the bold was becoming a little more "me!" I could feel myself getting more excited each week to try the next color. There was less apprehension about and less time spent wondering if I would feel the need to judge myself.

In fact, the last week of the month felt a bit of a let-down. I felt like there was a little bit of a halt in the progress of growing bold. It was a struggle to wear a less bold color that week, and I believe it contributed to me feeling less bold in myself.

I like having a bolder side. I like the life and energy that have been coming with it. I am looking forward to getting back to bold next week!

April

Week 1: REVLON – TRENDY (*green*)
Week 2: REVLON – PROVOCATIVE (*orange*)
Week 3: SINFUL COLORS – ENCHANTED (*purple*)
Week 4: SALON PERFECT – TRAFFIC CONE (*bright orange*)

April, Week 1
REVLON – TRENDY (*green*)

I think it is safe to say that after a week of "BLAH," I was ready to GO BOLD again! To begin this month, I started with a beautiful greenish color! It was becoming apparent that Revlon was emerging as one of my favorite brands. The colors were great and the quality of the polish was one that I could count on lasting pretty much the entire week without chipping. This green color was fun to wear. It felt professional, adventurous, and a breath of fresh air from the previous week! It was also festive for this week of Easter, even though I can honestly say that the holiday did not play any role in my selection process! I chose this color simply because I wanted to choose this color! The boldness was back and so was I!

> *I chose this color simply because I wanted to choose this color!*

April, Week 2
REVLON – PROVOCATIVE (*orange*)

This color was not a huge departure for me as I had worn similar colors on my toes for years and, I still do. But, to wear orange on my fingernails was a bit different. I remember feeling that this would have been a bit bold "back in the day" of several months ago. This time, however, it actually felt tame. It's funny how intention changes perspective. I have always liked the orange/red colors for pedicures. Now, it has graduated to manicures as well! I don't feel the need to keep my boldness hidden! That is awesome!

It's funny how intention changes perspective.

April, Week 3
SINFUL COLORS – ENCHANTED (*purple*)

Purple is my favorite color! So, I was excited to give this one a try! I must say it was quite bold and definitely not a color that I would have ever worn 4 months ago! I actually experienced a little bit of personal shock and awe with it! I had a lot of professional commitments throughout the week and, each time, I would think to myself, "Well, here we go! Hope this goes okay!" Wearing this purple in front of professional colleagues was a little unnerving until I asked myself, "What's the worst that will happen?" Any answer that I could think of was themed around the judgement, perception or thoughts of others. This was a great opportunity for me to realize that, no matter how well we know ourselves or think that we know others, judgment is always possible. And, ultimately, so what? Why let the potential of being judged derail the commitment I made to myself? That's BOLD right there!

...there is always room for the potential of being judged.

April, Week 4
SALON PERFECT – TRAFFIC CONE
(bright orange)

All I can say is boldness breeds boldness! This is the boldest, most obnoxious color that I have ever worn. I did have a professional "excuse" for wearing it. In my weekly networking group, we have to give an elevator pitch for our business. This week, instead of giving our own, we gave a pitch for another member. The member whose pitch I did worked for a company with an orange logo. So, I wrote a poem mentioning orange and dressed up in orange as well, including this nail polish! While the task was a bit of a crutch for wearing this bold color, it was also a chance to go really bold! The true challenge was wearing the polish throughout the week! Turns out, I enjoyed this color. It was bright and an attention-getter, which was a bit uncomfortable for me as I don't like to draw attention to myself. But, I wore it...and it was good!

Boldness breeds boldness!

Parting Thoughts

April was not only a bold month but it was also a fun month. I felt bold. I felt fun. All of this felt amazing! I would have never thought back in January that I would have four weeks that looked so bright and colorful. Every week had its own excitement. It was almost like a new adventure each week with unlimited possibilities.

These colors were great for me! I found myself gravitating only toward bright colors at the time of a new polish purchase. Who knew that would be the case?! Four months in and I do believe that this challenge is changing how I view myself and my opportunities. Can't wait to see where next month goes.

May

Week 1: NYC – BROADWAY BURGUNDY FROST (*burgundy red*)
Week 2: REVLON – GRAY SUEDE (*tan*)
Week 3: REVLON – CHOCOLATE TRUFFLE (*brown*)
Week 4: REVLON – CHARMING (*lilac*)

May, Week 1
NYC – BROADWAY BURGUNDY FROST
(burgundy red)

This color was similar to some other colors that I had worn so far with one slight difference: it had a shimmery frost cast to it. Normally, I don't care for the frosty colors. It's not that I feel they are too bold for me. I simply just don't prefer them. I thought I would give this one a try, though, since it was a richer color and one that I would tend to like as a non-frosty shade. It actually looked pretty good. There was just enough frost to add a little pizazz to the color but not too much to overdo it. I guess sometimes going bold means not always being sure about the moment yet realizing that it is a valuable part of the journey nonetheless! As for this color, I have to say that it wasn't one of my favorites but it would do for this week of the journey.

…sometimes going bold means not always being sure about the moment…

May, Week 2
REVLON – GRAY SUEDE (*tan*)

This was my least favorite color by far! I thought it was going to be another "chic" color like "Satin Ribbon" from week 2 in March. Instead, it looked dull and really took down my energy level. Surprisingly, out of all of the colors that I struggled to feel comfortable with, this one created the most struggle for opposite reasons. It was boring. It was not bold. The week, itself, was significant as well. My good friend and I were organizing our daughters' high school graduation party. A lot was changing and moving forward. I felt that this color was in direct contrast, like it was holding me back. By mid-week, I had to change the color! I couldn't take it! But, I didn't want to introduce a new color at this point. So, I looked through all of my polish and chose "Fashionista" from January, Week 4. Almost immediately, I felt reenergized! Ultimately, this was a battle between the boring and the bold. And, the bold won!

A lot was changing and moving forward...felt like it was holding me back.

May, Week 3
REVLON – CHOCOLATE TRUFFLE (*brown*)

After last week's color turmoil, I decided to take a step back and repeat a color. I had been buying a different nail polish every week for 19 weeks but I decided that last week was a sign that I needed to regroup. I wanted to start the week with confidence knowing that whatever color I chose I would keep on for the entire week. It was a little surprising to me how one tough week could shake my confidence a bit. But, it did. So, I wanted to try to build in more of a guarantee that this week would be successful. I struggled with the decision to not buy a new polish. I didn't want to set myself up for settling for repeat colors again. I don't like to settle…I like success! But, I went with my gut instinct and chose "chocolate truffle" – the color that smells like chocolate. This was a good decision, helping to keep me feeling grounded, in control and empowered as we were in the midst of yet another significant and emotional week with high school graduation approaching.

It was a little surprising to me how one tough week could shake my confidence…

May, Week 4
REVLON – CHARMING (*lilac*)

Ah! Back to a new color and one that worked for me and for this challenge! While this color was not a bright color, it was a new color for me and it worked well. I actually felt refreshed and energized from it even though it was a softer hue than many of the previous colors. It had a calming effect which was appropriate and needed given the past couple of weeks we had with all of the graduation stuff. It felt like a good spring color, too. This color was a good way to end the month because it restored confidence in myself and my selections. I felt an unexpected self-relief as if it was letting me know that everything was okay. We had made it through a very emotional time of high school graduation. I felt calm as I realized that not only did things go well, but from this point of change forward, everything was going to be okay.

I felt an unexpected self-relief as if...everything was ok...

Parting Thoughts

May was an up and down month when it came to color selection. This seemed to be a mirror image of the up and down nature of the month emotionally. Our oldest child was graduating high school, and my emotions were all over the place. My energies were all over the place. And, as noted, the nail polish colors were all over the place. Not only were the colors all over the place, but looking at the colors for the whole month of May compared to April's colors, it looks like maybe I retreated back just a bit in the overall boldness. I think, again, this was probably due, at least in part, to all that was going on this month. Maybe on a subconscious level I needed some familiarity in the midst of so many unknowns.

In the end, things came together on all fronts and finished strong. This is a great reminder to me that, through it all, we are stronger than we think and more capable than we often are willing to see. Sometimes, we just need to take life as it comes, knowing it is going to be challenging yet, at the same time, knowing that we can manage and will manage – and will do so better than we expect!

June

Week 1: REVLON – NAUGHTY (*purple*)
Week 2: REVLON – SHEER PINK
Week 3: REVLON – URBAN (*navy blue*)
Week 4: REVLON – CHERRIES IN THE SNOW (*red/pink*)
Week 5: RIMMEL – TEAL BLUE

June, Week 1
REVLON – NAUGHTY (*purple*)

May ended with a shade of purple, and June began with a shade of purple. This color was more of an earth tone and one that I really liked. I wondered this week how nail polishes get their names. Of the three shades of purple that I have worn to this point, the names have gone from "enchanted" in April to "charming" in May to "naughty" in June. Is there some kind of subliminal messaging going on with these names? Do these names influence how one feels, be it the one wearing the polish or the one observing the polish? These were interesting questions to me. Regardless of any truth behind the name, I liked wearing this color and felt empowered while wearing it. It felt rich, powerful, and professional!

I ... felt empowered...

June, Week 2
REVLON – SHEER PINK

This color was very similar to "Satin Ribbon" that I wore the second week of March. I found this brand to be smoother and to look a little better than the March brand. I had the same basic feelings that I had back in March in that this color made me feel chic and stylish. I also noticed that in addition to wearing jewelry that complimented the color, I began coordinating my clothes with my nail polish. I did this a little over the months. This particular week, however, I found myself wearing clothing colors that I thought enhanced this sheer pink, colors like light pink, chocolate brown, and cream. I liked how I felt even more put together from a fashion perspective as the clothes, jewelry and nail polish created a finished ensemble. I think that coordination will continue as the colors continue to change!

*I liked how I felt
even more put together.*

June, Week 3
REVLON – URBAN (*navy blue*)

I loved the name of this polish and the color of it! I love the color navy and loved wearing it on my nails! I felt powerful, trendy, and downright cool the entire week! There was a lot going on this week personally and professionally. I had corporate workshops to lead, professional meetings to facilitate, clients to see, and the week ended with attending college orientation with my daughter. This was a big week! And, I felt ready and excited for all of it! Wearing this color gave me a little extra pep in my step and I found myself thinking that I couldn't wait to wear it again! I think this color will end up in my top picks!

I felt powerful, trendy and downright cool...

June, Week 4
REVLON – CHERRIES IN THE SNOW
(red/pink)

This color was fun to wear. It was a change from the other reddish-pinkish colors that I had already worn. It was brighter, fresher, and felt like it added more life to the week. This was the fourth of four colors by Revlon this month. I have found that I have gravitated toward the Revlon brand a lot throughout this challenge. Revlon is a good quality brand with a middle-of-the-road price point and has the best variety of colors. I think when it is all said and done, there will be more Revlon colors in this new nail polish collection than any other brand. This color was fun and fresh. I felt fun and fresh! I enjoyed wearing it.

I felt fun and fresh!

June, Week 5
RIMMEL – TEAL BLUE

This was a new shade of blue, different from the other bluish, greenish, teal-like colors that I had already worn. It was also the only non-Revlon brand for June. It was fun to wear. I was finding that I tend to gravitate toward the blue tones of nail polish which was funny to me because before this nail polish adventure, I don't think I had ever worn any shade of blue nail polish! But, now, it was becoming a regular selection. Besides last month, there was at least one bluish, greenish, teal-like color every month! Like Revlon was becoming my "go to" nail polish brand, it looked like the blue/green colors were becoming a definite part of my bolder "go to" color wheel. Funny how when you stretch out of your comfort zone, sometimes you find a new part of yourself!

...when you stretch out of your comfort zone...you find a new part of yourself.

Parting Thoughts

June was great! I felt like I was back in the game after coming through everything last month. I enjoyed every single color this month, and would be excited to wear any of them again! The colors were vibrant, varied, and provided a sense of power and energy that seemed to fit with the first month of the summer. Each color had its own personality and each color felt like a good fit for me.

I didn't have any apprehensions or undesirable feelings toward any of the colors. It felt like they offered the right combination of professionalism, youthfulness, intrigue and boldness! As a result, I felt an extra boost of professionalism, youthfulness, intrigue and boldness! I think boldness and I are bonding!

July

Week 1: COVER GIRL – NAVY #307
Week 2: REVLON – VIXEN (*maroon*)
Week 3: REVLON – OPTIMISTIC (*pink*)
Week 4: SCANDED – BROWN ICE

July, Week 1
COVER GIRL – NAVY #307

Navy again! For some reason, this color provides me with a lot of motivation! This week, there was an overlap of time when my kids were at a church youth camp and my husband was out of town for work. I was missing all of them but I was motivated to get a lot done for work and at the house. I was also spending some time letting the creative juices flow as I brainstormed new ideas to move some things in my businesses forward. I really believe that this navy nail polish contributed to my energy, my motivation and my overall sense of feeling grounded and productive! It was a great way, and color, to start off the month!

...I was motivated...

July, Week 2
REVLON – VIXEN (*maroon*)

This was a repeat color from March, Week 1 and, again, I felt great wearing it. In the first week of March, I wrote, "...I was growing in my boldness!" Back then, I was entering the third month of this boldness challenge. I had experienced a number of uncomfortable moments as I was making these intentional efforts to go bold. It was an up and down process of emotions and thoughts, and by that first week of March, I felt that I was "growing" in that process. Now, two weeks into the seventh month, while I am still "growing," I would say what's more true is that the boldness has become a more integral part of who I am "becoming." I am not exactly sure what this means in terms of how it will impact me and play out in my life. But, I feel that I am at a new level of confidence, security and boldness than I was before. I can't quite put my finger on it but there is just something a little different!

...I am at a different level of confidence, security and boldness within.

July, Week 3
REVLON – OPTIMISTIC (*pink*)

I tend to stay away from brighter shades of pink. As you can see, any pink that I have chosen has been light or sheer. I don't wear bright pink. I don't own any bright pink clothes or accessories. If I am shopping for something new, I don't gravitate toward pink. So, choosing a bright pink color is completely out of the norm for me. But, it was time to try it! I did not think I would enjoy wearing this color because, I mean, what would I have to coordinate with it? Surprisingly, I liked it! I especially liked the name "optimistic!" Once I saw that name, I chose to focus on that rather than the color itself. But, the color did not disappoint! It was fun, cheery, and a breath of fresh air. I had anticipated that I would revert back to the "early days" and hide my nails in a little bit of embarrassment for wearing such an unfamiliar and bright color. Turns out, that was not the case at all! This was a great color!

It was time to try it!

July, Week 4
SCANDED – BROWN ICE

We know how much I have loved wearing the color brown. After a week of bright pink, I was ready to come back to a bold yet more familiar color this week. I didn't want to go back to the "chocolate truffle" that I had already worn since I had already repeated a color this month. So, I found another brown color of a different brand. This one, though, didn't have the same strong, bold impact as the previous brown color. It was watery in texture and I had a hard time getting the coats to look even. I had committed to this color both in money and mind. So, I made it work. After a day or so, I added another coat of the color and that seemed to help even out the coloring and make it a little stronger. It wasn't great but it was better. My insight this week was that sometimes going back to the familiar is not really as helpful as we might anticipate. Maybe it's just better to keep moving forward!

...the familiar is not really as helpful as we might anticipate.

Parting Thoughts

July was a strong month of color. Apart from the last week of the month, the colors were vibrant, had pizazz, and brought about an added sense of motivation for me.

It felt good to move out of the color comfort zone with the bright pink for the first time. I did wonder if I hadn't gone so bright, would I have felt better about the final brown color. Maybe having gone so bright just made the brown feel that much dimmer. It gave me something to consider because if that was the case, then what I experienced during the last week may have been less about the drab nature of this brown color and more about my continued growth in boldness. If this is true, then I am glad that the brown seemed to pale in comparison to the other colors! Ah – perspective!

August

Week 1: SALON PERFECT – ESCAPE TO NEVERLAND (*green*)
Week 2: POP-ARAZZI - TROPIC TANGO (*orange*)
Week 3: POP-ARAZZI – BREAK THE HEART (*purplish*)
Week 4: REVLON – FLIRT (*pink*)
Week 5: INSTA-DRI – NAVY FLEET (*navy blue*)

August, Week 1
SALON PERFECT – ESCAPE TO NEVERLAND
(green)

It was time to jump back into bold! It was also time to jump back into a new year of school for our son and for one of my two businesses. This business is an afterschool dance and fitness program for children ages 3-12. When school starts, we start! I figured if I am going to be jumping, I might as well jump bold with my nail polish, too! This bright green color was definitely a color that, previous to now, I would have never chosen, except maybe for something like St. Patrick's Day. It would have seemed too bold and obnoxious. But, I didn't feel any of that! I was excited to try this color. It was getting harder to find a color that felt new and bold enough. I had been noticing this one for weeks. So, I tried it - and it was great! I loved wearing it and felt energized from it. While I never would have worn this in the past, I was thrilled to do so now!

I felt energized!

August, Week 2
POP-ARAZZI - TROPIC TANGO (*orange*)

This color and next week's color I bought at the same time at the drugstore. When I saw the nail polish display, I thought these bottles were really different than the ones at Walmart where I bought all of the previous polishes. Before I go any further talking about this color, this might be a good place to pause and spend a few moments talking about my process during this nail polish challenge.

I am a huge process-oriented person. For me, process is at the heart of success, failure, and everything that exists in between. If I am going to be successful, then I will put into place a process that can bring about that success. I can want something, hope for something, expect something, even commit to something. But, if I don't set up a process to bring that "something" about, then there is a greater chance that I won't experience that "something" to the best and fullest possibility.

So, my process for this nail polish challenge so far has gone like this:

1) Visit the cosmetics section of our neighborhood Walmart on the weekend.
2) Walk up and down all four or so of the aisles that hold the various nail polish brands, remembering to check the aisle endcaps that hold more nail polish displays.
3) See what color catches my eye or jumps out at me.
4) Walk back through the aisles to see which other brands have similar shades of whatever color has spoken to me.
5) Compare the shades/brands.
6) Select the color for the week and purchase it.
7) Polish my nails with the new color on Sunday evening or sometime on Monday.
8) Wear the selected color all week (Tuesday-Sunday night or sometime on Monday).
9) Back to step 1.

I did not "plan" this process at the beginning of this challenge. It evolved over the first few weeks and has remained. So, buying nail polishes from a drugstore was not within the typical process for me. I only made nail polish purchases from

Walmart. However, for this particular week, it was a matter of convenience. I was already at the store purchasing office items and I knew that the weekend was going to be busy getting ready for all of the "back to school" stuff. As a result, I veered off course and changed the process, purchasing not one but two bottles of nail polish at a store other than Walmart.

> *... process is at the heart of success, failure, and everything ... in between ...*

All of this process talk is to say that I was excited to see something different than what I had become used to. It felt exciting to see different nail polish bottles and brands. I was excited to try these new polishes. What was reinforced to me in the end, which I already believed, was that process works. This nail polish, was just okay. I liked the color, but the texture was a challenge. The polish went on inconsistently. It would almost fade out as the coat was drying. I worked harder by putting on about 4 coats of polish before it looked even. While this polish was convenient to purchase and seemed exciting, it ended up being difficult to use. I worked with it during the week and I did enjoy wearing the orange color. But, unless next week's color works differently, I will return to the process that I know works well. I will find myself back in the cosmetics aisles at Walmart.

August, Week 3
POP-ARAZZI – BREAK THE HEART
(purplish)

I was looking forward to getting back to a shade of purple as you know purple is my favorite color. This one was almost a blackish-purple which was going to be a little different for me, too. Unfortunately, I had the same frustrating experience as last week in terms of the "process" of applying the polish. Once I got the color on and it was working better, it was a good and bold color to wear. I have learned several lessons over the past two weeks. First, convenience is not always convenient. Second, if the process is working, leave it alone. Third, process impacts outcome. And, finally, hang in there – there will be glitches to even the best of processes. Take a breath, make the best of what is available, and then find a way to make it better.

If the process is working,
let it continue working.

August, Week 4
REVLON – FLIRT (*pink*)

Ahhhh!!! Back to Walmart. Back to Revlon. Back to process. And...back to PINK? Who knew that it would be a bolder shade of pink that would bring about a sense of familiarity and relief! I really liked this shade of pink and just felt that it was so pretty. It was not as bold as the last pink that I wore but it was much more noticeable than the sheer pinks. It brought about a sense of beauty and femininity that I hadn't really felt or noticed from the other colors. That is not to say that some of the other colors were not beautiful or feminine. It just means that there were other qualities that stood out for me from those colors. This one, though, was pretty. It felt good wearing it. It was a great feeling to feel pretty and powerful at the same time.

> *It was a great feeling to feel pretty and powerful at the same time.*

August, Week 5

INSTA-DRI – NAVY FLEET (*navy blue*)

This was a new brand of nail polish for me. Truthfully, after a couple of weeks of going outside of my process, I was a little reluctant to try something new too soon. I have to say this choice was awesome! It was different. It was a smokier shade of navy. The brush was thicker and wider than most brushes This polish was bold with a little mystery. It opened up another level to this challenge, making me think that sometimes with boldness comes a bit of mystery. I found myself becoming more intentional about paying attention to the mystery of the week's happenings. I took notice of ordinary things and was able to notice more significance. I had conversations with people and was able to hear deeper meanings. This was a great opportunity to remember that what we experience is highly dependent upon our awareness of what is around us, and that within the ordinary, there can exist a deeper level of meaning and mystery.

Sometimes with boldness comes a bit of mystery.

Parting Thoughts

August was the most up and down month since May. It started strong, hit some rough patches, and then ended strong just like May. Looking back, it kind of all makes sense. We were preparing to get our daughter moved in to college, which was to happen at the end of week two. Interesting how this was right in the middle of the rocky patch of the nail polish challenge. Wow! I didn't even realize this until just now. Life was unsettled, and my nail polish journey was unsettled at the same time. I think the fact that I didn't realize this at the time is significant, perhaps an indication that I was trying not to think about our daughter leaving for school, but it was surfacing anyway. Also interesting to me is that the color selection for that week was orange, which is the color of her college. The power of process and the power of the subconscious mind seemed to be in alignment here.

This reflection highlights the connection between what goes on with us emotionally and what plays out in our lives. Maybe an insight here is that instead of trying not to think about what's tough for us, we can acknowledge it, embrace it, and do the best we can with it. We can do it!

September

Week 1: INSTA-DRI – CINNA-SNAP (*deep red*)
Week 2: SALON PERFECT – LILACKING CONTROL (*lavender*)
Week 3: LA COLORS – ELECTRA (*pink*)
Week 4: SINFUL COLORS – SNOW ME WHITE (*white*)

September, Week 1
INSTA-DRI – CINNA-SNAP (*deep red*)

I loved this color! It was a deep brick red and it was another color from the Insta-Dri brand that I had just discovered last week. I loved everything about this color. It looked good, it felt good, it had a cool name, and it went with everything. After an up and down month of August, I can say that this week felt like everything was getting back on track! This is a good thing to know and remember for the future – that when we are going through new experiences that are inevitable, even if they are ultimately good experiences, it can still be tough to process them and feel confident that we will make it through. When we find ourselves coming out on the other side, we find that we move right back into life, and we can pick up where we left off in a good, strong and bold fashion!

...everything was getting back on track!

September, Week 2
SALON PERFECT – LILACKING CONTROL
(lavender)

Back to purple with this lighter shade, it was similar to "charming" from week four in May. I enjoyed wearing it and didn't mind that it was a repeat color. I actually had forgotten that I wore a lavender shade already, and am continuing to notice that it is harder and harder now to keep track of which colors I haven't worn. That is kind of funny to me given that, prior to this nail polish challenge, I could have probably recited from memory the colors of polish that I had worn in my lifetime. It's amazing how being intentional and consistent, even about what seem to be small things like nail polish colors, can add to and enhance your life in ways that are big and significant!

...being intentional and consistent...can add to and enhance your life...

September, Week 3
LA COLORS – ELECTRA (*pink*)

This was a new brand for me and definitely a new color! Remember the "optimistic" pink from July week three? Well, this one was even bolder than that one! Why I end up choosing bold pink is beyond me. But, they work! The name "Electra" definitely fit this color as it was a little shocking to wear! I didn't find myself shying away from it at all, though. I was just surprised that it was as bright as it was. It felt fun and care-free to wear. The care-free feeling was good for me because I am a pretty structured, organized person. Like I said earlier, I am a process person. Being care-free is not a natural part of my process. I know that and I am okay with that. Wearing this color made me more aware that being care-free can work within my process.

The care-free feeling was good for me...

September, Week 4

SINFUL COLORS – SNOW ME WHITE (*white*)

French manicures? Yes! White polish on the entire nail? Probably not! I am not sure that I would have chosen white on my own. This week, though, there was a special reason to do so!

A special reason. My second business is my private practice where I provide counseling, life coaching and hypnosis to children, teens and adults. One of my child clients shared recently that she would be wearing all white the next time she saw me because she was raising money in a "white out" against cancer. So, I thought that this white nail polish would be great to wear. It was new for me and it fit my client's mission. It was touching to see a child with a heart for helping others while she was struggling in her life. Her boldness inspired my boldness! When she saw my nail polish, she thought I was cool. I thought she was amazing!

Her boldness inspired my boldness!

Parting Thoughts

September was awesome! It was a month of power, inspiration and boldness on so many levels. The colors each seemed to have their own personality! It was like a different party every week!

Speaking of parties, September was also my birthday month. I turned 49. I have to say that I have never really felt as old as the number of years that I hold. Turning 49 was no exception. So far, this entire nail polish challenge has helped me embrace so many new things about my life and the life that exists around me.

I am thankful for this birthday and am so grateful for all of the experiences that this year has brought to me through this challenge so far. September was an awesome month. I know that 49 is going to be an awesome year!

October

Week 1: ICE – SCREAM (*blue-green*)
Week 2: REVLON – CHOCOLATE TRUFFLE (*brown*)
Week 3: INSTA-DRI – PETAL PUSHER (*pink*)
Week 4: INSTA-DRI – BLACK TO BLACK

October, Week 1
ICE – SCREAM (*blue-green*)

I realized when I was shopping for my color for this week that I hadn't worn any shade of blue or green during September. I decided to make my first color of this month just that! I went back to look at how I felt in January and February when I wore a shade of blue or green, and it was amazing to see the difference of how I felt this week. Back then I felt self-conscious and uncomfortable with this type of color, even to the point of feeling the need to hide my fingers in certain settings. But, this week I didn't feel that at all. I didn't even feel it when we went out of town for the weekend to see many, many people that we hadn't seen in years. I felt confident and secure in this bold color choice and I wore it proudly with no trepidation. It is really something to see how your thoughts, outlook, perspective and even self-judgments can be transformed through intentional choices and commitments.

...self-judgments can be transformed through intentional choices and commitments.

October, Week 2

REVLON – CHOCOLATE TRUFFLE (*brown*)

It is obvious by now that this color is a favorite of mine as this is the third time that I am choosing to wear it this year. I wore it back in the third week of January and again in the third week of May. Part of my reason for repeating it here was that we had been out of town over the weekend, and I didn't have time to purchase a new color prior to the new week. I guess I could have purchased a new color earlier in the week last week so that I would have it. But, I didn't think of it at the time. And, I guess I could have made a polish purchase on Monday and started this new color a day or so late, but, I didn't want to start late. So, I went back to this favorite. Funny how one of my favorites is a color that I had never worn in my entire life until this year. To me, this was a great insight in that if we allow ourselves the opportunity to go bold, we open ourselves up to new things that can enrich our lives that, otherwise, we might have never known!

...go(ing) bold...can enrich our lives!

October, Week 3
INSTA DRI – PETAL PUSHER (*pink*)

I was excited to wear this color! Although it looked VERY similar to "Satin Ribbon" from the second week of March and "Sheer Pink" from the second week of June, I just had a feeling that this one would look or feel a little different. It did! The hue of the color was about the same as the other two, but the look of it was very different. While the other two looked like typical polish, this one looked a little more like paint. I felt like I had actually painted my nails. It was very cool. Every time that I typed on my laptop, or texted on my phone, or wrote down something on a post-it note, my nails just looked super cool! I felt cool and chic at the same time! I loved wearing this color and showing it off wherever I was and whatever I was doing.

> *I felt cool and chic at the same time!*

October, Week 4
INSTA DRI – BLACK TO BLACK

This was it - the week for the color that I had been avoiding all year long! Every time I saw it, I would ask myself if I would ever be bold enough to wear it. For some reason, black represented the boldest color of all. Why? I am not sure. Maybe because, in my mind as a child, black nail polish represented heavy metal music which was not my preference. Maybe because, in my mind as a teen, black nail polish represented depression. Maybe because, in my adult mind, black nail polish "seemed" unprofessional" But, I made the purchase! As I walked out of Walmart with that polish in hand, I surprisingly found myself feeling super excited. I couldn't wait to put it on! As I polished each nail, I was filled with feelings of inner self-pride that I had actually done something that I thought I would never do. WOW! To say that I loved wearing this color is an understatement! No matter where I was or what I was doing, I felt proud of myself! I felt bold!

I had actually done something that I thought I would never do.

Parting Thoughts

October was amazing! I took on my biggest nemesis when it comes to nail polish colors, and we became best friends. That probably sounds silly but it's true. This month was a great example of doing what I felt led to do without reservation or fear. When I look back at some of the events that took place in my life this month, I can see that I had added confidence to take initiative in areas where I might not have done so. I had the ability to stand up for or ask for things that I needed that I might have otherwise let go.

While this nail polish challenge has been an external exercise of boldness, I can see the internal impact that it is having on me. I wouldn't say that it is changing me. I would say that it is allowing me to be more of who I am meant to be.

November

Week 1: ORLY – ECHO PARK (*green*)
Week 2: COVER GIRL – WINE TO FIVE (*maroon*)
Week 3: COVER GIRL – MUTANT (*blue*)
Week 4: ICE – CAN'T STOP (*orange*)

November, Week 1
ORLY – ECHO PARK (*green*)

We all know what happened when I went outside of my process for shopping for polish back in August but, I decided to try it again! In Target one day, I saw a display of ORLY nail polish. My eyes were drawn to this green color. It was pretty and I thought the bottle was cute. Of course, I learned the last time not to judge a nail polish by its bottle. This time, though, it worked out! This polish had a unique look and feel to it, almost like liquid rubber. The texture caused me to take more notice of my nails through the week. This made me realize that I had not been taking as much notice of my nails like I did in the first months of this challenge. On some level, I wondered if the novelty of this may have worn off. Maybe, though, the bolder colors just felt more natural for me now. Either way, what I think it means is that what was once just an idea to go bold had now become a part of my life, a part of my lifestyle, a part of me!

What was once simply a thought...had now become a part of my life...

November, Week 2
COVER GIRL – WINE TO FIVE (*maroon*)

This color was a little surprising to me. I thought it was going to be a deep shade of maroon but it was a bit lighter than what I had anticipated. I liked it, though, because it felt light and airy. It was bold but had a gentleness about it. I think that kind of fits me. I don't have an abrasive personality. I don't think anyone who knows me would say that I am harsh. I think people see me as a person who is gentle yet assertive. I like those two qualities together. I think this boldness challenge has helped to develop, even more, some of the assertive side of me. It has helped me embrace on a deeper level that being assertive, especially about the things that I may need, is okay!

> *This boldness challenge has helped...the assertive side of me.*

November, Week 3
COVER GIRL – MUTANT (*blue*)

I was expecting this color to be a little brighter and bolder since it looked like an electric blue. Like the color from last week, it was a little milder, but it was fun to wear. It felt very trendy, cool, hip, and, professional all at the same time. I guess last week and this week have been good examples of the idea that bold does not always have to be "in your face" bold. Being bold can be subtle and strong at the same time. That was a pretty cool insight as it seemed to bring together, maybe for the first time, who I have always been with who I am growing to be through this challenge.

> *Being bold can be subtle and strong at the same time.*

November, Week 4
ICE – CAN'T STOP (*orange*)

I chose this color on purpose as this was Thanksgiving week and I thought orange was a great Thanksgiving color. Again, in keeping with what seemed to be a theme this month, it was also a little lighter than I thought it would be, but, it was pretty. It had sort of a calming, soothing effect. I found myself reflecting this week on so many things and feeling such a deeper sense of gratitude for all of these things. Not that I haven't been grateful in the past. But, I think I was just more aware of so many aspects of so many things and was overwhelmed with gratitude. I guess being more intentional and aware on a daily basis gives you more things to be grateful for in the long run.

Being more intentional...gives you more to be grateful for...

Parting Thoughts

November was a month of surprises! It was surprising to me that making changes in the process actually worked out okay considering the tough time I had with it back in August . It was surprising how what was once so new and different now seemed common and natural. It was also surprising to me how my expectations about what colors would look like ended up not being accurate each time.

In addition to these surprises, I felt a little surprised by the deeper level of gratitude I was feeling during the Thanksgiving season. I generally operate from a perspective of gratitude. I tend to look at the glass half full and look at what I have versus what I lack. I think an overall takeaway from this month is that being intentional in going bold can lead to deep levels of growth and gratitude no matter where we are on the gratitude spectrum. There is always room to be more thankful.

December

Week 1:   REVLON – KNOCKOUT (*black*)

Week 2:   RIMMEL – PLAZA PLUMBERRY (*dark plum*)

Week 3:   REVLON – POSH (*green*)

Week 4:   INSTA-DRI – RAPID RED

             INSTA-DRI – GRAPE SHIFTER (for Christmas)

Week 5:   INSTA-DRI – NAVY FLEET

             SINFUL COLORS – TEAL MIDNIGHT (for New Year's Eve)

December, Week 1
REVLON – KNOCKOUT (*black*)

I can't believe it! This is the first week of the last month of the year! And, what better way to start it out than with my number one color coup! Yup – it was back in black, baby! And, it was Revlon, which turned out to be one of my top two brands of the year! This was a true winner in every sense of the word! December is always a fun and exciting month with all of the Christmas festivities. Wearing black for this first week made it even more festive. That may sound strange and, given my preconceived perceptions about black nail polish that I shared when I wore it back in the fourth week of October, I would never have thought that I would say that black nail polish adds to the festivities. Going bold changes things!

Going bold changes things!

December, Week 2

RIMMEL – PLAZA PLUMBERRY (*dark plum*)

At first, this dark plum color looked like it wouldn't be too far off from black. I had second thoughts about wearing a color so similar to the week before. When it went on the nails, though, it was definitely different. It was plum, for sure! It felt festive as well as I kept thinking about "Twas The Night Before Christmas" and the "visions of sugar plums." To say that I felt good or bold now seems cliché, but it is true. I can't even imagine going back to the colors that I used to wear prior to this year. I wouldn't even feel like I was wearing any polish of any significance. Bold is where it is at when it comes to polish, and life!

I can't even imagine going back...

December, Week 3
REVLON – POSH (green)

I decided earlier this month that I would take the week before Christmas and the week after Christmas to wear green and red to be festive. This week was the green. It was definitely green – bright green – fun green! This time last year, I might have worn a color like this and would only have been able to because of the holiday. But, this year was different. I was bolder. I was wearing it for me first and the Christmas holiday second. It's amazing what a difference a year of intention can make!

It's amazing what a difference a year of intention can make!

December, Week 4
INSTA-DRI – RAPID RED
INSTA-DRI GRAPE SHIFTER (for Christmas)

It's Christmas week! So exciting! I chose the second of my top two nail polish brands to celebrate. Not just one color in this brand, but two colors. And, not just two colors, but one of them glitter! Yes! Boldness at its highest! I wore the red polish for the first half of the week and then added the glitter on top of the red for Christmas Eve through the rest of the weekend! How fun! I loved every minute of this week for so many reasons! Adding glitter gave that extra spice to the already festive red. I was feeling it! What an amazing month and year! With just one more week to go, I find myself reflective and a little emotional as 2015 comes to a close. Many developments have occurred in recent months that I made an initial reference to in the introduction of this book. I will give updates on these in my closing remarks. Until then...we have a lot of celebrating to do!

I was feeling it!

December, Week 5
INSTA-DRI – NAVY FLEET
SINFUL COLORS TEAL MIDNIGHT
(for New Year's Eve)

The last week of 2015! It seemed fitting to wear an "old" color and a "new" color. I chose navy blue from August, week 5, and this blue glitter, wearing navy first, and adding the glitter for New Year's Eve and through the rest of the week. I loved this! It was festive, bold and beautiful! I felt amazing wearing it and hated the thought of changing it next week. Then, it hit me! What about next week?! It will be 2016. My year-long nail polish, go bold challenge will be over. What am I going to do? Will I still buy nail polish? I can't imagine "buy nail polish" not being on my weekly "to do" list. All of this made me realize that the new year brings with it lots of reflection, questions and unknowns, too. 2015 has been amazing! Who knows what 2016 will be like. But, I believe it will be awesome!

*...the new year brings
...reflection, questions
and unknowns...*

Epilogue

It is hard to believe that 52 weeks have just about come and gone. While I had never been much for making New Year's resolutions, this year I actually did something specific and different for an entire year! I made an intentional commitment to myself and I stuck to it for the whole year. This was big! This nail polish challenge started out as a simple idea, a way to create an intentional change in my own life while the lives of others around me, and life itself, would be changing in major ways. But, it became so much more.

Changes that we had been anticipating in 2015 for the members of our family all happened. Our daughter graduated from high school, selected a college, and began her freshman year. Our son got his driver's license and began driving himself to all of his commitments and activities. My husband decided to leave his full-time corporate job to accept the full-time position of senior pastor at our church. The Mastermind Group of like-minded business professionals that I had initiated and facilitated went strong all year as each of us experienced growth and success in our businesses and, as a result, we extended our commitment to each other for the 2016 year.

At the beginning of 2015, all of this change was coming. By the end of 2015, all of this change had come. And, it was all good!

Through all of these changes, I continued to change my nail polish. Every week, without fail, no matter what was happening or where our family was in the midst of all of these life transitions, I remained committed to the nail polish.

After taking some time to process this commitment that I had not only made but also kept with myself FIFTY-TWO WEEKS, I began to realize that changing my nail polish did more than provide me with an opportunity to be intentional. It did more than give me a greater and more varied color palette of nail polishes. It did more than move me out of my comfort zone. The impact was far greater!

Before we get to some of these impacts, let's take a look at what that nail polish box looks like now, 52 weeks later:

Do you remember what the initial box of nail polish looked like? Here's a reminder:

This simple and intentional challenge yielded some deep and complex insights for me, the impact of which will remain with me forever. Here they are:

Changing my nail polish each week gave me opportunity to see how much I tend to judge myself. There were definitely days and weeks where I had to sit with my self-judgment, move past my self-judgement, and work hard to not let that self-judgment take over. While I was struggling off and on with judging myself, I was realizing more and more that, most of the time at least, as I am hyper-aware of what is going on within me, others have no clue. While I was stressing over what others might think of my color of the week, not one person seemed to be bothered enough by my choices to address them with me. More than likely, few people, if any, were paying enough attention. That was quite freeing for me as I continued to realize that the main, and probably only, person judging me was me.

Changing my nail polish each week helped me develop a greater level of empathy for my clients, especially around the issues of self-confidence, making decisions, giving ourselves grace, and building ourselves up rather than tearing ourselves down. It helped me to realize, even more than usual, how making changes in our lives is not easy as it takes daily and consistent action, attention, and intention. I feel I generally have a pretty good instinct and intuition around what it is taking for others to hang in there and manage their lives. By dealing with my own struggles related to this boldness challenge, I realized how much effort it can take for someone who is struggling to get out of bed in the mornings every morning, or to believe in themselves when the chips are down.

Changing my nail polish each week provided some challenges when I ended up not liking the color selection. Some of those weeks were tough. It was tough to hang in there when I felt dissatisfied. These tough times were opportunities for me to prove to myself that I can push through struggle more than I realize, building up my sense of personal power and resilience.

I am not one to easily give up. I rarely, if ever, give up when I have made a commitment to someone else or something outside of myself. I will find a way to see the commitment through to the end, regardless of the challenges. If the commitment is strictly to myself, however, I have to be honest and say that, if the struggles seem too big or too out of my wheelhouse, I can be tempted to give up or at least question whether or not to keep going. This challenge forced me to stay committed to me. Nobody else knew about it. Nobody else was going to benefit from it. It was all ME! At some point, I had to decide that I was worth pushing through any struggles that came up!

Changing my nail polish each week brought out more of my fun, playful, silly side. Even though I am a kid at heart, as an adult, it is easy to feel the need to act like an adult! Adults are supposed to be professional, appropriate, role models, good examples, productive, etc. I think it is possible to be all of these things and be FUN, too! Sometimes, we need the reminder that it is okay to view the world through the eyes of a child. We can be carefree. We can jump in the puddles. We can be optimistic. We can color outside of the lines. We can see the best in others. We can believe in possibilities. Most of all, we can have fun and make the most of every day!

Changing my nail polish each week brought out my bolder side. I would say that, as a general rule, I am an assertive person. I have thoughts and opinions and am willing to state them and stand my ground in a gentle and calm manner. However, there are times when I question or wonder if I should act on what I think, feel or believe, especially when there are more aggressive personalities in the room or if I perceive there is a real risk that I might be judged or rejected. In these situations, I might shy away from myself for the moment. I will usually come back to the issue, even specifically addressing it with the more aggressive people; but, it may take me a moment to do so. This challenge helped me see more clearly that there is no reason to shy away from myself but, instead, there is every reason to be true to myself even, and especially, if it means taking risks to do so!

Changing my nail polish each week kept my attention on being intentional each and every day, which brought deeper meaning to each day. In my line of work, being present and mindful is critical! I have to listen to my clients as they share their stories. I have to read between the lines to understand what they are really saying, or meaning, or feeling. I have to be observant of their body language, their facial expressions, etc. I am trained in and skilled at being present and mindful. However, in the busyness of regular life, I can often lose track of being present to the moment of the day. What I have been reminded of is that real meaning is found in the moments – big moments for sure but also in the smallest of moments. It is the small moments that may carry the deepest or most lasting insight or experience. I remember one day during this challenge year, I was very aware of the breeze outside. It was a beautiful, sunny day. As I was walking from my car into Panera, I noticed the gentle breeze. This definitely was not the first breeze I had ever felt. But, being intentional about taking it in moved me to the choice of sitting outside instead of inside that day. I rarely sit outside if I am at Panera to get some work done because I am often working on my laptop and need to be near an electrical outlet. On this particular day, with this particular gentle breeze, I decided to abandon the work I needed to do on the laptop and just enjoy the gift of the beautiful weather. That day, while it was only one day, changed my perspective for the long term because, now, whenever it is a beautiful day, I notice it and stop for at least a few moments to embrace it!

Changing my nail polish each week provided me with a structured and scheduled opportunity for weekly self-care. It is so easy to put our self-care on the back burner. Sometimes our self-care doesn't even make it onto a burner. By having to pause each week for an hour or more to prepare and polish my nails for the upcoming week, it was a way to keep self-care on the front burner. As I placed intentional effort on caring for myself, I realized that I was even more energized to care for others. I like investing in others. It comes naturally to me. It is not usually a chore or burden or obligation. It is what I would choose to do. What I found, though, was that by investing in myself on a consistent and regular basis, I could invest even more in those who matter to me! Being structured about the self-care through the nail polish, I found that I was adding other structured and consistent self-care to my schedule. The main one was, and still is, a regular exercise schedule, 3 mornings a week plus a bonus weekend workout when the weekend schedule allows for it. The overall lesson for me is that self-care yields more self-care and greater care for others.

Changing my nail polish each week afforded me opportunities to succeed at going outside of my comfort zone. This allowed me to overcome moments when I was self-conscious and to grow in my confidence. I don't normally sit around thinking about my level of confidence. Like most of us, my confidence waxes and wanes depending on the issue, situation, etc. When you step outside your comfort zone, those areas of lacking confidence creep up with greater presence. As I noted in some of the weeks, some of the colors that were outside my comfort zone brought to light my own self-judgment, my perceived judgment by others, and even called into question some of my values around professionalism and being a grown up. Throughout this journey, what I realized was that many, if not all, of these perceptions and values come from our upbringing, our life experiences and our understanding of the world around us. This means the boundaries we place on ourselves are constructed as well. We have the power to move those boundaries to be open to, and to include, new and exciting beliefs, experiences, actions and ideas! We are only bound by our comfort zone if we allow ourselves to be!

Overall, I would say that this nail polish challenge didn't really change me but, instead, it brought out more of who I am and who I am meant to be. It allowed me to be creative, current, expressive, intentional, thoughtful, mindful, a planner, etc. etc. – all qualities that I have but maybe don't always use toward myself or to the fullest! This nail polish challenge also allowed me to enhance my perspective of daily life. There are always things in our lives that we would rather not have to deal with, that we are afraid to deal with, or that we are unsure of how to deal with. There are always days that we would just rather write off as bad days and try to move forward. This nail polish challenge helped to remind me that we have the power, each and every moment, to make the most of what we have and pour ourselves into the strengths and gifts that have been given to us. This challenge allowed me to be more grateful for life itself.

Because I loved every minute of this nail polish challenge of going bold in 2015 and found the entire experience invaluable, I continued to change my nail polish every week in 2016 and am still doing so today. I am not necessarily buying new colors every week. I am still using the nail polish left over from last year. I have actually bought a few new bottles here and there.

My 2015 journey brought me through many life events and brought me to much personal insight and growth. That is why I wanted to share my journey with you. My hope in writing this book is that you will find something of value within my journey that might motivate, inspire, and encourage you toward something that will mean something for your life - something which you can be intentional about that challenges you to be more of you! Perhaps a journey like this will, without realizing it at the time, help you stay connected to your personal strength and power through the many ups and downs that life throws your way. It might not be through the weekly changing of nail polish, but, I believe there is something that will bring intention, purpose and meaning to your days in a little bit of a different way.

Thank you so much for reading about my nail polish journey. I would love to hear your feedback! There are a couple of ways that we can connect:

Facebook – visit, "like," and leave comments on our Facebook page at <u>Go Bold The Nail Polish Challenge</u>.

Email – you can email me anytime at my counseling practice email: <u>amy@goboldnailpolishchallenge.com</u>. I look forward to hearing from you! Can't wait to hear about how you decide to GO BOLD!

About the Author

Amy Head, LCSW, was born in Boston, MA. She earned her BA in Philosophy from Furman University and her MSW from The University of Louisville, Kent School of Social Work.

Amy is the owner of New Perspectives for Life, LLC, in Marietta, Georgia, where she provides counseling, life coaching, and hypnosis for children, teens, adults, couples and families. She also works with corporations, bringing her services on-site to the employees in order to enhance their emotional and mental wellness. Amy serves as keynote speaker and seminar presenter for corporate, church and community events.

Amy is also the founder of Cardio Kool Kids, Inc., a comprehensive dance and fitness program for kids ages three through fifth grade. Cardio Kool Kids goes on-site to preschools and elementary schools, getting kids excited and skilled in a variety of dance and fitness formats!

Amy lives in Marietta, GA with her husband, Kevin, and their two children, Jenna and Joshua.